THE VO-TECH
TRACK TO SUCCESS IN
BUSINESS

Adam Furgang

ROSEN
PUBLISHING

New York

Published in 2015 by The Rosen Publishing Group, Inc.
29 East 21st Street, New York, NY 10010

Library of Congress Cataloging-in-Publication Data

Furgang, Adam.
The vo-tech track to success in business/Adam Furgang.—First Edition.
        pages cm.—(Learning a trade, preparing for a career)
Audience: Grade 7 to 12.
Includes bibliographical references and index.
ISBN 978-1-4777-7722-0 (library bound)
1. Business education—Vocational guidance—Juvenile literature.
2. Success in business—Vocational guidance—Juvenile literature.
I. Title.
HF1106.F794 2014
650.1—dc23
                                                                2013051151

Manufactured in the United States of America

CONTENTS

INTRODUCTION

I magine sitting in your social studies class and listening to your teacher talk about business entrepreneurs like Thomas Edison and Bill Gates. You might suddenly perk up a little. Some students might perk up more than they remember ever perking up in class before. Sometimes students never really think about how some businesspeople can change the world. But these entrepreneurs did something that appeals to some students. They figured out how to bring the new technologies of their time to the public. If you ever thought businesspeople were boring, think again, and imagine the possibilities that face people who explore new ideas. You may find that people frequently ask you about what you want to do when you grow up. Maybe you were never sure. Perhaps you can't imagine that anyone your age could know what he or she wants to do years from now.

But your mind may now think of a business career in all new ways. Think about what an inspiration Sheryl Sandberg, Facebook's chief operating officer, is to young people, often young women, who want to go into business. Sandberg is one of the most powerful women in the business world, and many young women admire her hard work. You may not expect to be the next Sheryl Sandberg, but what if you could become involved in the business world and make an impact on people's lives? There is a lot to learn about business, although you may

Sheryl Sandberg, chief operating officer of Facebook, has been an inspirational business leader for many people entering the business world.

not even be sure you want to go to college after high school, let alone major in business. You may wish there was a way to explore your ideas while you are still in high school. You may wish there was a way to get some experience in the real world to figure out what you want to do.

If you were to talk to your teacher after class, he or she might recommend that you get involved in the school's vocational-technical, or vo-tech, program. Instead of only an academic experience in high school, a vo-tech program would allow you to gain real-world skills that would make you valuable to an employer right after high school. The program has several paths that students can choose based on their interests. If you chose the business path, you would spend part of your days in class and part of them working in a real business environment. That's an exciting thought. You could actually get some real business experience while you are still in school.

If you set up an appointment with your guidance counselor to talk about the possibilities, you may be even more interested. Many vo-tech programs are also called career and technical education, or CTE. That makes sense, too. Why not get an education in careers? It will prepare you for life after graduation, regardless of whether it is immediately after graduation or after a two-year or even a four-year college program. Entering a vo-tech program now could help you start learning life skills you will eventually use on the job. The possibilities are endless for a student who wants to start career training early.

Chapter One

GETTING STARTED IN CAREER AND TECHNICAL EDUCATION

You may have heard of vo-tech training, or vocational-technical training. The programs have been around for decades in high schools across the country. Over the years, vo-tech training has prepared countless students for careers they could jump into right after high school. It has also prepared students to enter more specialized career training after high school. Some courses even prepared students to enter education programs after high school, such as two-year technical schools or community colleges.

But somewhere along the line, vo-tech programs gained a reputation for being only for people who are interested in learning about car mechanics or a career working with their hands. That could not be further from the truth. Today vo-tech education is referred to as career and technical education, or CTE. It focuses on many clusters of possible careers. Students interested in business can learn about management and administration. That means learning about how businesses are run. Other possible

Vo-tech education may also be referred to as career and technical education, or CTE. Students have sixteen different career clusters to choose from and explore.

careers in the business area include marketing, sales, information technology, and computers.

In addition to business, students can explore health sciences, education, arts and communications, architecture, transportation, hospitality, and tourism. Even law, public safety, agriculture, food, government, and human services are possibilities. This opens up opportunities for students who are motivated and ready to try out new things to get on the career path early. According to the Association for Career and Technical Education, there are sixteen different career clusters to explore and more than seventy-nine pathways for study. That gives great options to high school students when you consider that more than two-thirds of America's young people are not likely to graduate from a four-year college. Consider also that a four-year college does not necessarily prepare students for the skills they need for the work force. Many companies request that employees have certain skills that are not taught in four-year colleges. They request computer, administrative, and technical skills that are taught in CTE programs.

The research shows that CTE programs provide students with skills that prepare them for work. According to the Association for Career and Technical Education, 81 percent of high school dropouts who were surveyed say that they would have stayed in school if their education included real-world learning opportunities. For students concentrating in CTE programs in high school, the graduation rate is 90.18 percent. The national average graduation rate is just 74.9 percent. CTE programs make many students want to learn more after graduation, as well. More than 70 percent of high school CTE students went on to further training and education shortly after high school. So how does a student get involved in a career and technical education program?

Think It Over

Before jumping into a program, think about what your interests are. Someone who enjoys the idea of the business world has a lot of opportunities to explore.

BE AN EARLY BIRD

Even a person in middle school can think about his or her interests. Most middle schools offer clubs that focus on business, such as an entrepreneur club or a finance club. Banking programs are also offered at many schools to teach students about money and finance. Some middle schools also have exploratory courses in technology and math that can help students learn practical skills. These are all helpful activities and experiences to get involved in if you think you may be interested in a CTE program when you get to high school. Keep your eyes and ears open for opportunities that appeal to you. There may be more of them than you think!

Economics and banking can both be specializations for people interested in business. Think about your interests and become aware of the kinds of programs available to you.

Think about whether you would like a career in which you work with people or if you would prefer to work with technology. This can greatly affect the kind of program you should choose and whether you would enjoy the program. If you would like to work with people, for example, think further about what you would like. Does the idea of sales interest you, or would you be interested in interviewing and hiring people for a job?

If you're not sure about what interests you, there is plenty of time to explore. In fact, the programs are set up so that you have time to learn about a wide variety of careers. Programs for ninth and tenth graders offer introductory courses. Students spend time learning about a particular field. They don't need to choose a particular path that interests them most. They spend time learning about how the different parts of the field work together. In programs for eleventh and twelfth graders, more specialized and advanced instruction is given. Students may work in a field that they would like to learn more about.

Don't worry if you think getting job skills in high school will make you unprepared for college if you ever decide that you would like to attend a two-year or four-year college down the road. CTE programs provide a balance between academics and job skills. This is meant to prepare students for either a job after graduation or a college career. This kind of preparedness makes you look attractive to both an employer and a college. The college sees that you understand the importance of real-world skills, and the employer sees that you can handle academics as well.

When you get out of high school, the job training gets more and more specific and prepares you for jobs that are in demand and require skills. Many employers have trouble finding employees. This happens even in a time of slow economic growth, such as a recession. Employees are required to have certain skills that employers don't have time to teach them on the job. Many college graduates don't have these real-world technical skills. It's students who have gone to technical training programs, such as CTE programs, who get these jobs. Some of them are high paying and in demand. Information technology is an area of business that requires training and skills.

Grab Some Help

Once you have decided what kind of career path might interest you most, talk to a guidance counselor about the opportunities your school can provide to help you reach your goals. A counselor is someone who can answer your questions and help you learn about possibilities you had not considered. You might meet with a guidance counselor by yourself or set up an appointment so that your parents can attend as well. A guidance counselor's job is to prepare students for the future. This means that the counselor is aware of many programs and how successful they are for different types of students. Don't be afraid to ask for help and get the counselor's advice. At the very least, get a counselor to answer your questions.

A guidance counselor can let you know what the requirements are for the CTE program and whether

Take advantage of the resources your guidance counselor can offer. A counselor can point you in the right direction if you need more specialized help.

you might eventually work in the field in a hands-on position. By telling the guidance counselor your interests, he or she may be able to recommend something for you to explore. A counselor may also recommend books that can help you learn more about fields of study, such as business.

Don't forget to ask a lot of questions. Write them down so that you don't forget when you see the guidance counselor. Ask your parents or guardian for other examples of questions that you may not have thought of. Remember that you are planning your future, and there is nothing more important than that. Specify that you are interested in business, and your counselor will be able to narrow down his or her responses to be as helpful as possible. Someone who is interested in the arts or in health may get an explanation of a different program than someone who wants to go into the field of business.

After you have gotten some basic information from the counselor, think about a follow-up visit. You may have been overwhelmed after your first meeting. You may wish to take some time to do research. Then you might have another list of questions that are more specific. Meeting with your counselor again will show that you are serious about looking into the program. Find out how to enroll and what permission papers or health papers may be required. Listen carefully to the instructions about the paperwork and enrollment, and get the required signatures from a parent or guardian before deadlines.

Some states even have high schools that specialize in CTE programs. Your guidance counselor can let you know if you live near one of these schools. Specialized vo-tech high schools have proved to be very effective for students who are looking for hands-on, real-world skills. In New Mexico's Loving High School Career Clusters Model program, students have an on-time graduation rate of about 95 percent. In Massachusetts's Tri-County Regional Vocational Technical High School, about 92 percent of students graduate. That's higher than the average graduation rate of conventional high schools. And many of these specialized schools have a great percentage of students who continue on into college or later return for adult education classes.

Get Out in the Field

One of the most rewarding and anticipated parts of a CTE program is the practical experience that it gives students. Instead of staying in the classroom all day, students get to work in local business offices, much like real employees do. This is possibly the most exciting part of the program, but it requires that students be prepared to act professionally. Many business offices have dress codes that they also expect CTE students to follow. Be sure to follow all guidelines that you are given. Take the Job seriously and always act professionally while on the job. You may be able to make a good impression on an employer. This may even lead to a recommendation or a job when you graduate.

Working in the field is the practical experience that draws most students to a CTE program in the first place. Remember also that you will still be required to go to

As a vo-tech business student, you may be assigned to work in the field in a business office, gaining experience during the work day and school day.

school and continue your academic studies. Some CTE programs might have students work in the field one full day a week. Others might have them in the office only for a couple of hours in the afternoons. The rest of the time is spent at school in classes. Grades are also expected to be kept up, even on workdays. Sometimes finals or state tests are required during times when the student would normally be on the job. Students and their advisers may have to adjust work schedules with an employer to meet school obligations.

Chapter Two

BUSINESS PROGRAMS

For students who are attracted by the idea of working in the business world, there are plenty of opportunities in vo-tech programs. Getting a head start on career skills can be done in many ways. There are about a half dozen career pathways to consider in the area of business. Two of those will be discussed in this chapter—business administrative support and business management. These two broad areas can prepare students in many ways to work in offices and get the skills they need to succeed.

The business world can be confusing. Many people don't understand the difference between the various areas of focus in the business world. Business administration and business management are two of the most commonly confused areas. Simply put, business administration prepares a person to handle the day-to-day workings of a business and its operations. Business management prepares people to lead and spearhead new ideas in business. A person in business management may be more of an entrepreneurial idea person. Business management specialists may

High school students in a vo-tech business program will learn about both business administration and business management. Think about what interests you most!

need the assistance of business administrators to carry out their plans and make them successful. The two specialties work hand in hand. People who choose to go into one of these areas should also be familiar with the other area. They should think about what their goals in business might be and what kind of personality they have. Someone who is more detail-oriented and organized might succeed in business administration. Similarly, someone with creative ideas or strong problem-solving skills might consider business management. Keep in mind, however, that there is a bit of overlap between the two areas, and it helps to use all your skills and develop new skills to truly succeed in business. Business managers should never assume that they don't have to do business administration duties. In the same way, business administrators should not think that they don't need to think critically or creatively on the job.

When a vo-tech, or CTE, student goes out on the job, he or she might be asked to work in a variety of office settings. Working in a business office might require working side by side with an office secretary or assistant, doing daily tasks that keep the office

RISING THROUGH THE RANKS

The jobs that may attract a business management student may not be available until the student gets many years of practical experience in the business world. That does not mean that the business management classes in a CTE program are not valuable. The courses help to make students think in a more critical way about business and help them to understand how vast the world of business is. It is common for someone to graduate from school and be an administrative assistant, then rise through the ranks slowly. That person may start a career as an administrative assistant but end up as an executive.

running. A student may learn computer skills on the job, such as updating or managing Web site information. A student may also learn communication skills, such as talking to clients or answering correspondence. The day-to-day work adds up to experience and real-world skills that employers can use.

In the school environment, classes may be offered that add to the typical high school academic education. Vo-tech business training can involve academic courses that help students understand the importance of business training.

Business Administrative Support

A business administrator needs to develop knowledge of the entire business process. Luckily, with career and technical education programs, this learning can start as early as high school. When entering a CTE program, there are required classes that students must take to make sure that they learn the essentials of their field. Some of the required credits needed for study in business administrative support include business communications, computer technology, digital business, and word processing.

Business communications is such an important part of the field that there may be several classes to take. No business can be successful without good communication among team members and with outside clients, customers, or partners. Skills needed for good business communication include professional writing and speaking skills and training in technologies that allow people and groups to communicate with

A tech-savvy person can excel in the area of business communications. Meetings and presentations rely on technologies that are constantly changing.

each other. Conference calls, e-mails, business meetings, and trade conferences are all examples of ways that businesses and business associates communicate with each other.

Computer technology is another important part of business administrative support. Although computer technology changes frequently, students must become familiar and comfortable with computers.

CHANGING YOUR MIND

One of the benefits of a vo-tech program is that you can explore a sector of business and decide whether it interests you or not. Many four-year college graduates can't tell whether they like working in a field until they graduate, find a job, and begin working in it for a while. A CTE student can experiment with different aspects of the business before even graduating from high school. Through their on-the-job experiences, students may also learn about other opportunities they never knew existed in the field. With CTE programs, there is time while you are still young to change your mind about what you want to focus on.

Today's businesses rely on communication through computers. Digital business technologies are also an important part of changing businesses. Mobile communications and conferencing technology fall under the category of computer technology and digital business. Understanding how communication tools work for a business is very important. The business cannot run without modern computer technologies. That technology is needed for both communication and for marketing and advertising the business.

Another skill that a business administrative support student might learn about is accounting. In order to stay in business, companies must manage their money and keep track of their profits and spending. Accounting is the process of keeping track of financial accounts, or records.

Business law is also helpful for someone to know in the business administrative support field. There are many local, state, and federal laws that businesses must follow. Courses in business law can help someone who is not a lawyer make sense of these laws and understand what they mean.

What can people who take business administrative support classes expect to do with the skills they have gained? What kinds of jobs are available to them after graduation? One of the most common jobs is an administrative assistant. This person supports a higher-level manager in the company by answering phones, responding to mail, making travel plans, and making the boss's workload lighter. Great communication and organization skills are needed for administrative assistants.

Other jobs include an office manager, who takes care of the day-to-day activities in an office environment. These tasks may include ordering new office supplies, taking care of seating arrangements, or training new employees about company policies. He or she is the person most employees go to with a question. Office holidays, sick days, office breaks, and other employee details are often worked out through the office manager. An office manager is a highly organized person and should have a strong ability to get along with people.

In addition to these jobs, some business administrative support students may go on to work in human resources departments that hire new employees. They might work in desktop publishing to put out company newsletters or other materials. They might also work as customer service assistants, who speak directly with customers and help address their questions or complaints.

Business Management

A business management student would take different CTE courses than a business administrative support student. The course load would focus on some other aspects of the business. For example, marketing is one major difference between the two fields. Marketing is the action of promoting or selling goods or services. This can include advertising or market research. Business management students study marketing as part of their training. Successful marketing can mean the difference between a successful company and an unsuccessful one. Marketing often means coming up with clever ideas to make your product stand out above others that are similar to it. Marketing also means understanding who your audience is and appealing to them. Additionally, it can mean researching and finding out from customers how your product can be better.

Business management students might also expect to take some courses in business law. When someone is in a position in business to make decisions for the company, it is important to understand what decisions might not be allowed based on the law. Business law can help to guide executives so that they know their

Market research involves talking to the public and understanding how customers use and think about products.

limitations. They might learn about laws for hiring employees. They might also learn about laws for selling goods in different states or countries. While businesspeople are not expected to be lawyers or experts in the law, it helps to become familiar with the basic laws that govern a business.

Classes in digital business applications can also be expected for business management students. That means learning about how businesses use technology to operate. Today a business needs to communicate and function digitally, so understanding digital programs is important.

What can a person who specializes in business management expect to do after high school? One possible job is a market research assistant. Market research involves talking to the public to get their feedback on the company's products or services. A market research assistant may be responsible for getting feedback from customers or individuals who sample, review, or comment on their products.

A public relations assistant works in the department that oversees how the company is perceived by its own clients and also the media. The job may involve downplaying negative publicity or providing interviews with the media. People with good communication skills and a professional demeanor are needed for the public relations department.

An e-commerce assistant works in the department that handles the company's electronic business. That means overseeing and managing the company's Web systems. Organized people who are comfortable with computers and technology would be good working in an e-commerce department.

Chapter Three

FINANCE JOBS

In addition to business management and business administrative support, many vo-tech business programs have a focus on finance. Money is the backbone of any business and the reason that a business may fail or succeed. Without the people who figure a business's finances, a company may go out of business quickly. Finance specialists can make a lot of money in their careers, and people who like to do this type of work can be very happy in the business environment. But how can you tell if the field of finance is right for you?

Are You a Finance Type?

If you've always been good with numbers and problem solving, finance may be the career path for you. People who are suited for this technical and detail-oriented field are often very analytical. They are usually good at math and can solve some number problems in their heads.

If you're good with numbers and excel in math, a finance career may be worth pursuing through a vo-tech business program.

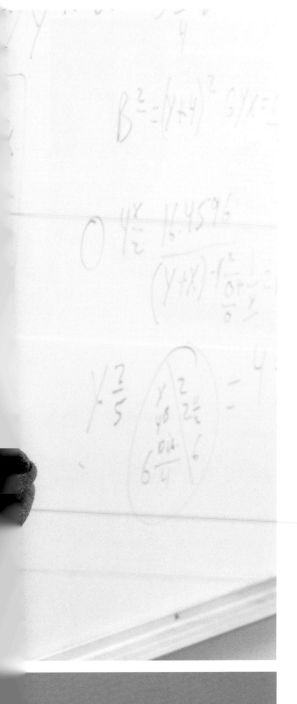

Even if good with numbers, a finance specialist definitely is not required to be a walking calculator. In fact, keeping accurate records and double-checking your work is an important part of the job. Some people consider this type of work to be difficult, but someone who has excelled in math classes can expect to do well in a finance career.

A person who would be good at finance is also likely to be conservative with money and aware of the ultimate goal of saving or making money for the company. The person might also like doing detail-oriented work such as calculations. Some people find this type of work to be very difficult, while others enjoy it greatly. When thinking about a specialty in the business field, it is

Computer programs can calculate complex data, but it takes a detail-oriented thinker to analyze the data and understand its implications in the business world.

important to think about your own personality and what you enjoy doing.

What Do Finance Types Do?

Part of the job is to compare the money a company earns with the money it spends. This can mean using complex computer programs that can help determine the profits a company might make on a product when

SALARY AND EDUCATION LEVEL ARE RELATED

Did you ever wonder why a company's chief financial officer makes more than the company's bookkeeper? It's true that the CFO has a lot more responsibility than the bookkeeper, but chances are that the CFO is much more educated, as well. According to the U.S. Bureau of Labor Statistics, a job requiring just a high school education will pay less than one requiring an associate's degree. Similarly, a person who has gone to school two or four more years to earn a bachelor's degree or a master's degree will get more money than a person with a lower-level college degree.

it makes the item at different costs. For example, a company may make a profit on a pair of jeans it produces. But consider how much more profit the company might make if the jeans were made out of a cheaper material and customers were charged the same price. You might think it would make an even larger profit. However, if the product is not considered to be good quality or worth the price, the customer may not spend the money to buy it at all. As a result, the company will not make the profit you expected. Instead, the company may lose money producing an item that does not sell. Hitting the right balance between the projected profits and losses of a company can be tricky. Many people are in charge of the process, but it is the finance department that calculates the differences between possibilities, using computer programs.

The head of a finance department is often a company's chief financial officer, or CFO. The CFO plays a large role in making financial decisions for a company. This person works side by side with other executives, such as the company's president or chief executive officer (CEO). Together they make decisions about what is best for the company and what will be best for its financial security.

A company's finance department also calculates the amount of taxes that the company owes several times per year. A tax is an amount of money owed to the federal, state, or local government. There are some finance specialists who focus only on tax matters for a company. These specialists keep track of taxes that are paid to employees and what percentage of money should be taken out of employee paychecks. They stay up to date on new and changing laws about tax codes.

Form **1120**
orm
Department of the Treasury
Internal Revenue Service

For calendar

A Check if:

1 a Consolidated return
(attach Form 851) .

b Life/nonlife consolidated return . . . . . .

Personal holding co
(attach Sch PH) . . .

2

Personal service
corp (see instr) . . .

3

Schedule M-3
attached . . . .

4

Print
or
type

E

1 a Gross receipts or sale

2 Cost of goods s

3 Gross profit. S

Understanding both federal and state tax laws is a big part of the
finance department's job in any company.

What Kinds Of Classes Should I Take?

The required courses that a finance specialist may expect to take in a vo-tech program mainly relate to math. Accounting, banking, and general finance courses are necessary to give students real-life skills that they can use on the job. Accounting classes relate to taxes and finances associated with taxes.

There may be several levels of accounting classes to take, including at the honors level if students qualify. Accounting may be the most important class for finance students not only because it explains information about taxes and how to calculate them for business, but because it helps students understand the effects that taxes have on a business. Students may also be able to stay up to date with tax software that can be used on the job.

While finance classes may be the most important courses for someone who specializes in the field, general business classes are also important. These classes give students a general understanding of the business world and help them find their true interests.

Working in an office during school days as part of the vo-tech program can give students a good sense of what the work might be like. Students can work in the office environment and ask questions about the type of hours employees put in at the job and what they like most about their jobs. Professional relationships that are started at vo-tech programs can help students make their futures brighter.

JOB GROWTH AND A LIFETIME OF LEARNING

There is high demand in the job market for people with finance skills. This is why continuing to learn and getting an education after high school graduation is so important. Most of the demand to fill jobs is for people who have two-year or four-year degrees. Even people who obtain entry-level degrees can continue to grow in their jobs and be promoted over time. Going back to school is a possibility for many people who start their careers right after high school. The most important part of learning is to never give up and to keep your mind open to always learning more and challenging yourself.

What Kinds of Jobs Can I Expect to Get?

In order to work in the finance field after graduation, finance students may need to do more than just work in the field. Getting further education is especially important for finance careers because they require technical skills, experience, and training.

Some jobs may be available right after two-year college programs, however. An accounting clerk is in charge of a company's financial records. This includes anything that is written or printed as hard copy or stored in a software or online database. The kind of

An accounting clerk may be hired with an associate's degree and may be able to be promoted within a company.

information might be payroll or other business transactions. This person might also be called a bookkeeping clerk or a financial clerk. The clerk has a higher-level supervisor who oversees the clerk's work. A clerk must be detail oriented and able to perform a variety of duties.

Even working in the finance or accounting department of a company will give a high school graduate good exposure to the business. Working as an administrative assistant to an accountant or financial supervisor can make a student or recent graduate aware of the computer software that is used and the difficulty level of the software.

Chapter Four

TECHNOLOGY AND E-BUSINESS PROGRAMS

One of the fastest-growing parts of the business field is in the area of technology and e-business. The people who graduated from high school or college just ten years ago are working in a completely different work world than today's graduates. The face of business has changed because of our new reliance on technology to do every part of our jobs. At the turn of the twenty-first century, it was rare to see a video conference call, let alone one that could be organized in minutes over the Internet. Most of the records of human resources or accounting departments have been digitized, and new records are likely kept in on-line databases. People who have not kept up with the changing technologies have difficulties functioning in the business world. While the technology was meant to make life easier, the software and applications may not be intuitive or easy for some people to learn.

The demand for skilled workers in the area of technology is very high, and it shows no signs of cooling down. These workers acquire the skills they need through special training. As a result, the salaries for technology workers in many companies may be higher than that of other employees.

People who work in this kind of field can expect to take courses related to the latest computer technologies. Getting out into the field and using the newest equipment and programs is sometimes the best way for students to practice. The hands-on aspect of technology education is often best when it is done in a practical setting. Many schools don't have the budgets to purchase a lot of computer software and constantly

Keeping up on computer and business education throughout your life is one of the best ways to stay ahead in the business world.

keep it updated with the latest versions. However, it is important that a business stay up to date, especially as the use of such programs helps make the company money. So you may find that people who work in a vo-tech or CTE environment gain very valuable experience when they work with an employer on their technical training.

Being an apprentice and taking on projects from employers puts students in the middle of the action. Some classes simply have students read books about how to use a computer program. Then the students take a test to see that they understood what they learned. But practical use in a professional setting is much more beneficial for the student. Some programs that offer vo-tech training ask students to take part in

STUDENT LEADERSHIP ORGANIZATIONS

Entrepreneurs and business leaders were often student leaders, also. Leadership skills can be gained at a vo-tech program or in your day-to-day school life. Look for chances to become involved in student groups. Business clubs and entrepreneur clubs give students a chance to gather and discuss their business ideas. Some organizations focus on leadership skills and help students develop the confidence and ability to lead their peers, preparing them for a successful career in business.

company projects. That means using the computers for practical purposes. If the student finishes the project successfully, that's proof that the student learned. Real life becomes the test for the student, and there are plenty of supportive teachers to help make sure the student gets through the training and gains confidence in his or her abilities. As with finance and other branches of business, the more education a person gains in technology, the better off he or she will be in the professional world. Here are some of the courses you can expect to take in a vo-tech program.

Business Technology Support

There are a wide variety of computer classes for people interested in technology. Web page design is one of the most creative endeavors with computer technology, and most technology students are encouraged to take at least one class in web design. While many companies hire design firms to make their company websites, it is often company employees who update the sites and add information to them regularly. This requires some knowledge of design and how to combine those design skills with software applications.

Desktop publishing is another area of computer technology that results in media that communicates information about a company. Desktop publishing is most often used for printed materials for a company, such as newsletters or advertisements. Students can benefit from classes or real-world experience that teaches about page layouts and how to produce an electronic file that can be printed on a large scale.

Business technology students are likely to have classes in computer technology. This is an overview of the kinds of computer programs and applications used in business. Computer programming may also fall under this category. Computer programming is the most technical aspect of computer technology. Programming is the customized work that goes into making a program or application. While computer programming is a degree that requires further education, it helps to have vo-tech students learn about the basics and consider whether it is something they would like to pursue further. Some computer programmers create programs based on specific needs and requests of the company, so the skills needed are very specialized.

E-business is a growing section of the business world and one that requires skilled workers. "E-business" is a term to describe businesses that are run on the Internet. Many traditional businesses also have an e-business division. For example, you may be able to go to a store at the mall and buy items, but you might also shop online for the same items. The online portion of the business is called the e-business. It requires its own technologies, its own marketing, and its own policies with customers and customer service. Someone who specializes in e-business must be very familiar with the computer technologies that make the online business run. That may include developing or understanding a backup system and a way to protect sensitive customer information such as credit card numbers or other personal information.

Students who specialize in e-business, or any computer technology aspect of a business, can

E-business is a fast-growing part of the business world. Online sales and other transactions account for a large part of today's business successes.

expect to continue with their education long after their initial vo-tech training. Computer technology is constantly changing, and businesses need to keep up with every change.

Changing a company over from an older computer system to a newer one is always a challenge, and patient and knowledgeable computer and technology employees are always needed to help make the transitions smoother. Helping employees with their computer problems is also a challenge, so technical

Each business must maintain modern technology systems to compete with other companies and communicate with customers.

support within companies is very important. People who have knowledge of new systems and how they might interact with old systems can be a very valuable part of a company. As with other parts of the business world, working on the job and gaining professional experience is very important for students learning about technology.

Entrepreneurship

There are two ways to think about business. You can think about either keeping a business running or creating a business with new ideas. One area of specialty in vo-tech business is entrepreneurship. A person who can harness a great idea and make it work is valuable to any company. In recent years,

REAL-LIFE ENTREPRENEURS

While it is recommended that students get as much of an education as possible, there are some entrepreneurs who did not take the traditional educational route. Some business entrepreneurs who did not go to or finish college include Facebook founder Mark Zuckerberg and computer whizzes Bill Gates and Steve Jobs, founders of Microsoft and Apple, respectively. Add to that list Virgin Group founder Richard Branson and Mary Kay Cosmetics founder Mary Kay Ash. Each person had a solid foundation in what makes a businesses successful.

many business entrepreneurs have emerged in the area of computers. That's because computer technology and e-business were new, unexplored areas.

Some of the more well-known business entrepreneurs include Mark Zuckerberg, founder of Facebook, and Larry Page and Sergey Brin, founders of Google. Pierre Omidyar, the founder of eBay, is another example of how a person can take a good business idea and turn it into gold. Some business inventions have changed the way we live and made our lives easier. Vo-tech programs that focus on entrepreneurialism help students to think critically and develop ways to explore their ideas.

This kind of program is good for students who have confidence in their great ideas but need to learn the skills to make their ideas become a reality. A wide variety of classes can help students prepare

Facebook founder Mark Zuckerberg turned his business into a multibillion-dollar enterprise.

for starting a small business or becoming an active part of an existing small business. Marketing, economics, finance, communications, and leadership skills are taught to students who are interested in entrepreneurship.

Entrepreneurs have engaged in all aspects of business. They may have a business idea related to art, computers, finance, music, sports, or any other field. Vo-tech programs help students learn the skills they need to turn their passion and ideas into good business sense.

Chapter Five

PUTTING YOUR BEST FOOT FORWARD

Becoming involved in a vo-tech program can be exciting for students. Some students who live in areas where vo-tech specialty high schools exist are fortunate to have the opportunity to have such great resources at their fingertips. But it is important for students to remember that simply becoming involved and having access to these resources does not mean that you will be guaranteed a good job or even that you will succeed. It takes constant hard work and determination to be successful in business, no matter what your early opportunities are.

According to the National Association of State Directors of Career Technical Education Consortium (NASDCTEc), there are fourteen million students enrolled in CTE or vo-tech programs in the United States. These students are getting an important opportunity to gain valuable skills in the real world. The skills meet a pressing need in the country, especially in times of poor or recovering economies. Andy Van Kleunen, executive director of the National

Skills Coalition, was quoted on the organization's Web site as saying, "For the CTE community, it's not a question of whether recovering industries like manufacturing or healthcare are ready to hire; it's a question of whether our CTE programs have enough capacity to meet that demand. We know there is a skills gap and we know that CTE programs can help fill it." This applies to business programs as well as other career paths in CTE.

When only 69 percent of students graduate from high school in four years, vo-tech options become more and more important. They seem to encourage students to enjoy learning and to work hard. When students don't graduate from high school, it means that they will likely be heading into a lifetime of lower pay. Lost education means lost money. According to NASDCTEc, about twelve million high school students are predicted to drop out of school in the next decade. That will mean a loss of $3 trillion in potential jobs that they could have obtained if only they had finished high school. NASDCTEc also states that students who stay in school, continue their education, and get degrees help fuel the economy. That's because these people become qualified to fill positions that are in need. CTE and vo-tech programs help encourage students to continue their education. The main reason that students feel the desire to move on with their education after one of these programs is that it helps give their education direction. As explained on the NASDCTEc website, Jennifer Davis, a graduate from a CTE program, was inspired by the program to continue her education.

Students in CTE programs graduate with skills that can take other students years to gain in the workforce.

She said, "I developed self-confidence that helped me through college and still helps me today."

That's why it's important to put your best foot forward and take the program very seriously. The work that you do in the program can help shape your future and the decisions you make. According to the NASDCTEc website, graduate Roger Thompson also felt inspired by the program. "My motivation and drive grew...I learned skills that are applied to my profession on a daily basis, which helped me succeed." To ensure that you get the most out of any vo-tech program that you enroll in, follow some of these tips for success.

Get on the Right Path

If you think you are interested in a vo-tech program, research the possibilities offered in your area as soon as possible. Some school districts have vo-tech programs. Others have entire specialty schools dedicated to vo-tech or career and technology education. A guidance counselor be very helpful to students who show interest. However, the details are up to the student. There may be deadlines for getting involved in the process. There may be permission slips or medical forms that have to be filled out for acceptance into the program. The student needs to keep on top of these responsibilities and be sure to carry through with what is needed.

Once in a program, scheduling can be a challenge for some students who are not used to keeping track of responsibilities. Be sure to attend all classes as well

GETTING A GED IF NECESSARY

Students know that they should be keeping up with school work and not dropping out of high school. However, the dropout rate remains high in many schools around the country. That does not mean that people who have dropped out of school will never have good professional opportunities open to them. At any age, the opportunity to get a high school equivalency degree is open to people who dropped out. The degree is called a general equivalency diploma, or GED. The best part is, someone can get this degree as an adult and still be working and earning money to pay for it.

The GED is an exam for people who did not finish high school. Passing the exam allows them to earn a high school equivalency degree.

as all of the on-the-job training sessions you are responsible for. Not only do you get graded on your work and participation in the program, but some employers come to depend on the work that students do. They need reliable workers who can also be responsible. When you are on the job, always be respectful to mentors who have dedicated themselves to helping you. Use a professional manner with people in the workforce as well as with other students on the job. Teachers or mentors who have to get involved with personal problems between students are not getting the best performance possible out of those students. If the relationships between students are a struggle, the experience will not be as rewarding as it should be. Make an effort to get along with other students. You will make a good impression on teachers and mentors.

Use Good Judgment

All vo-tech programs are different, but each of them requires that the students use good judgment. Students who run into problems either with teachers, on-the-job mentors, or other students should understand that they are not expected to handle their problems alone. If there is a dispute with a teacher that needs to be worked out, you can go to a guidance counselor for help. If a dispute arises between you and another student, or with an on-the-job supervisor, try talking it out with your teacher. If you feel that you are following all program rules and regulations but still end up with problems, you should seek out a proper way to solve the conflict. You want to keep your reputation positive and be sure that people understand that you are willing to play by the rules. The recommendations of the teachers and mentors you come across may be important after you graduate, so be sure to use good judgment and keep your experience on the positive side.

Forge good relationships with the people you come across in the vo-tech program. You may find that these people can help your career get on track and stay on track for years to come.

Choose a Mentor

One of the most beneficial things about a vo-tech experience is the opportunity to have a mentor who can teach you real-life skills. A mentor is someone who can teach you and guide you as you learn. Vo-tech mentors help guide students to apply the skills they learned in class to the real-world working environment. One opportunity is called job shadowing. This means that a student might spend a day alongside a company employee to see what the responsibilities are and what skills are needed to do the job. According to the New Castle County Vocational Technical School District in Delaware, students in mentoring situations develop better communication, leadership, and social skills. Students may continue these mentoring relationships after the program is over, as mentors may be willing to provide recommendations for jobs in the future. When prospective employers try to make their decisions about whom to hire, they often call references, people who can recommend the prospective

Working with a mentor can provide students with work skills as well as professional contacts for the future.

employee. It is important to choose a reference who thinks highly of your work ethic and your ability to take direction and learn new skills. Someone such as a mentor can give specific examples of ways that you excelled at a job. A mentor can give a good idea about your personality and help to convince a prospective employer that you are the right choice.

For students who do not have a specific mentor who has worked in a supervisory role, it may help to choose a teacher or guidance counselor as a job reference. Vo-tech programs look good to an employer who reviews a résumé, so someone who was involved in your vo-tech experience should be able to recommend you to an employer by giving real examples of how you learned about or experienced the business world as part of the program.

Be prepared for a prospective employer to ask you about your vo-tech experiences in an interview.

Keep Up With Schoolwork

Students in vo-tech programs are often dedicated to their work and feel excited about their future prospects. That sometimes means that students forget to pay attention to their regular schoolwork. It is important not to let classes slip in order to concentrate on real-world experiences. In fact, the way vo-tech programs have been changed in recent years places an extra emphasis on the importance of classroom education. The 2006 Carl D. Perkins Career and Technical Education Act, or Perkins IV, allows each state to create its own programs of study for vo-tech training. As a result, emphasis has been placed on going through classroom learning and making sure that a student's education is complete and well-rounded. By having classroom courses, the newer programs ensure that students will be comfortable if they decide to continue their education after high school. A large percentage of students decide to continue their vo-tech professional education in college or through adult education. That's why staying accustomed to classroom learning is important when going through a vo-tech program.

Chapter Six

YOU'RE NOT DONE YET!

Suppose you had a great experience in a vo-tech program and you gained wonderful real-life skills that you can use in the business world every day. What should you do next? You can certainly get a job and start earning money, but your lifetime of learning has only just begun. There are many more opportunities that you can take advantage of to help you have the best career possible.

Many career and technical education programs are so successful, students continue on in their learning. They realize that vo-tech programs are informative, useful, and a great benefit to their lives in general. At New Jersey's Newark Tech High School, 86 percent of their high school graduates report going on to two- or four-year colleges. At the Kearney High School Linked Learning Program in California, 95 percent of students report going to college after they graduate. Many of these students begin working in the field they already trained for and use the money they earned on the job to help them pay for their continued education.

RETURNING FOR ADULT EDUCATION

Many vo-tech training schools offer extensive adult education courses. These can be one-time courses for people who wish to gain skills for their job or for people who wish to learn skills to switch jobs. Many part-time and evening courses are available in adult education because many of the students are working full-time. Many courses even provide the same mentoring and apprenticeship work experiences that vo-tech high school students receive when learning skills useful for their profession.

Schooling doesn't stop with high school. Adult education is an important part of lifetime learning in business.

The vo-tech career path should be thought of as a continuing experience. According to NASDCTEc, vo-tech training continues to keep people up to date on career skills, even after they graduate. Vince Orza, a CTE graduate who now works as a marketing professor at the University of Central Oklahoma, says that CTE programs are "a career, path, or plan—with a method to get there." That means that the program will try to make you as ready and equipped for the working world as possible, then keep you up on how you can stay relevant in your field. "CTE does a great job of listening to the students and placing them in the career path that is best suited for their skills and passion," says CTE graduate Richard Hight on the NASDCTEc website. However, for a career path that goes past the high school years, you may need to consider going back for further training or education in your field. For some high school students, that means looking for colleges before you graduate. Here's how you can use your time while still in high school to try to grab an opportunity to further your education.

Find a Program

Just as you went to your guidance counselor for help getting into a vo-tech program, think about getting the counselor's help to research a program that can help you continue with your already valuable experiences. Counselors and vo-tech training teachers have a good sense of the programs that are available in your area. Use their knowledge to help you learn about what may be available to you.

KEEP LOOKING AHEAD

When thinking about what you would like to do in the professional business world, it helps to take a look at the Bureau of Labor Statistics website. The government agency allows users to search for job titles, provides job descriptions, and lists the skills required and the typical work environment. It also lists salaries for each job, based on averages throughout the country. The site is a valuable source for students who wish to research jobs and think about their future.

Also think about whether you wish to stay near home or go farther away for the program. Many vo-tech graduates begin working after graduation. Some work for the companies that partnered with their high school. That means that some high school graduates look for postsecondary programs close to home so they can continue to work part-time. Consider this when you think about where you will live when you go to school.

Look into both two-year programs and four-year programs in business. A full-time, two-year program generally provides graduates with an associate's degree. Community colleges offer good opportunities to earn associate's degrees, and the teachers may be familiar with the vo-tech programs that your high

Pursuing a business career can lead to success, promotions, and new experiences. Giving presentations is just one skill that business students must learn.

school or county offers. When you check out schools, research what their coursework is like and what kinds of hands-on experiences their business or technical training classes provide to students. Take a look at both the required classes as well as the elective classes, which are ones that students can choose themselves based on their particular major or interests. Look at any requirements that must be met before you can be accepted to the school, such as SAT scores and grade-point averages. Be sure you meet these requirements before you apply so that you do not waste time or money applying to schools that you may not be qualified for.

Four-year schools can be researched in the same way that two-year programs can be explored. Remember to go to your library or do some research on the Internet. Consider the kinds of schools that interest you, have good business programs, and are affordable. Consider whether you will be going to school full-time or part-time. This will affect the type of job that you can hold while going to school. It is difficult to work full-time while also going to college full-time. The reason is not only because there are not enough hours in the day to meet the obligations of both school and work, but you are not likely to be able to attend work full-time without having scheduling conflicts that will disrupt your workday. Ask your parents what you are expected to contribute in terms of financing. Each family has a different situation, and the possibilities for financing college are varied. Your family's individual situation should be considered as you figure out your price range and ability to finance your education.

Grab It

Once you have decided on some schools that interest you, it's time to get to work meeting all of the deadline dates and finding out about application fees for each school. Every school makes its own policies regarding fees, deadlines, and application requirements. It can be a challenge to keep up with every one, but you are more likely to be accepted to a school if you take charge of the paperwork and get it all done on time.

Most applications will require that the student write a personal essay. Be sure you give yourself enough

Spend time on your college applications, including the essay. Some vo-tech students might choose to discuss their work experiences in their essays.

time to write your essays, and be sure to proofread them carefully before submitting them.

Also keep track of the times when you are expected to hear back from each school and when each school semester begins and ends. This may affect your decision on which college to choose if you have to make a choice.

There are many opportunities available for students after high school. Students who graduate have the largest number of choices. If you've become part of a vo-tech program during high school, you have likely made very valuable professional connections that will help you get work right away. You could work for a while, then go back and get a higher degree on a part-time or a full-time basis. Even without a higher degree, there are plenty of adult education opportunities available for people who wish to continue gaining professional skills. Keep your options open because vo-tech and career and technology education can put endless opportunities at your fingertips.

accounting The action or process of keeping financial records, or records about money.

associate's degree A college degree that is typically earned after completing two years' worth of full-time classes.

bachelor's degree A college degree that is typically earned after four years' worth of full-time classes.

business administration A branch of business education that supports a balanced and broad approach to learning about how businesses work.

business management A branch of business education that concerns the planning, directing, and controlling of business operations.

CEO Chief executive officer; the highest-ranking corporate executive in a business.

CFO Chief financial officer; the corporate executive or officer in charge of managing a company's finances.

CTE Career and technology education; career or vocational training in school that prepares students for jobs in a particular kind of career, such as business.

e-business The commercial transactions that a company conducts electronically on the Internet; e-commerce.

economics The study of the way wealth is produced, consumed, and transferred.

entrepreneur A person who takes on financial risk to organize or operate a new business venture.

finance The study of or management of large amounts of money, especially by corporations.

GED General equivalency diploma; a degree that can be earned as an alternative to a high school education.

information technology The study or use of computer or telecommunication systems for storing, retrieving, or sending information.

job shadowing A program for students to find out what it is like to be in a particular profession.

mentor An experienced or trusted adviser to a younger person or student.

postsecondary Following high school.

reference A person named in a résumé or on an application to provide personal and professional feedback about an applicant.

résumé A list of academic and professional accomplishments.

vo-tech program A school or program designed to provide vocational and technical training and experience to students.

For More Information

Business Professionals of America
5454 Cleveland Avenue
Columbus, OH 43231-4021
(800) 334-2007
Website: http://www.bpa.org
Business Professionals of America is a career and tech-
    nical student organization for students interested in
    careers in business management, information tech-
    nology, and office administration

Canadian Federation of Students
338C Somerset Street West
Ottawa, ON K2P 0J9
Canada
(613) 232-7394
Website: http://www.cfs-fcee.ca
The Canadian Federation of Students was formed to
    help provide students with a united front to handle
    issues regarding their education such as tuition,
    financial assistance, and funding.

Canadian Student Leadership Association
Three Oaks Senior High School
10 Kenmoore Avenue
Summerside, PE C1N 4V9
Canada
(902) 888-8460
Website: http://www.casaaleadership.ca
This nonprofit educational association supports
    the growth of students as leaders. It provides
    resources, scholarships, and programs for mem-
    bers across Canada.

DECA, Inc.
1908 Association Drive
Reston, VA 20191
(703) 860-5000
Website: http://www.deca.org
Formerly known as Delta Epsilon Chi and Distributive
    Education Clubs of America, DECA is a student
    organization that prepares high school and college
    student entrepreneurs and future business leaders
    for careers in marketing, management, and other
    professional areas.

Future Business Leaders of America—Phi Beta Lambda
1912 Association Drive
Reston, VA 20191-1591
(800) 325-2946
Website: http://www.fbla-pbl.org
This nonprofit education association has a division
    for high school students interested in business
    careers, as well as a division for junior high and
    middle school students.

Junior Achievement USA
One Education Way
Colorado Springs, CO 80906
(719) 540-8000
Website: http://www.juniorachievement.org
Junior Achievement is a volunteer-based organization
    with K–12 programs designed to foster skills such
    as entrepreneurship, work readiness, and financial
    literacy, with a goal of getting students prepared for
    a global marketplace.

Skills USA
14001 SkillsUSA Way
Leesburg, VA 20176
(703)777-8810
Website: http://www.skillsusa.org
SkillsUSA is a student-teacher-industry partnership
  focused on providing students with the skills
  needed to compete in today's workforce.

Websites

Due to the changing nature of Internet links, Rosen
Publishing has developed an online list of websites
related to the subject of this book. This site is updated
regularly. Please use this link to access the list:

http://www.rosenlinks.com/TRADE/Busi

For Further Reading

Bingham, Jason. *Cultureship: The ACBs of Business Leadership.* Cambridge, England: Grove Books, 2013.

Butler, Tamsen. *The Complete Guide to Personal Finance: For Teenagers and College Students.* Stark, FL: Atlantic Publishing Group, 2010.

Carter Gray, Kenneth. *Getting Real: Helping Teens Find Their Future.* Thousand Oaks, CA: Corwin, 2008.

Christen, Carol, and Richard N. Bolles. *Discovering Yourself, Defining Your Future.* New York, NY: Ten Speed Press, 2010.

College Board. *Get It Together for College: A Planner to Help You Get Organized and Get In.* New York, NY: College Board, 2011.

Dorch, Patricia. *Job Search: Teen Interview Tips and Strategies to Get Hired.* New York, NY: Execu Dress, 2012.

Klaus, Peggy. *The Hard Truth About Soft Skills: Workplace Lessons Smart People Wish They'd Learned Sooner.* New York, NY: HarperBusiness, 2008.

Lore, Nicholas. *Now What?: The Young Person's Guide to Choosing the Perfect Career.* New York, NY: Touchstone, 2008.

Lore, Nicholas. *The Pathfinder: How to Choose or Change Your Career for a Lifetime of Satisfaction and Success.* New York, NY: Touchstone Books, 2012.

Mariotti, Steve. *Student Activity Workbook for Entrepreneurship: Owning Your Future.* Upper Saddle River, NJ: Prentice Hall, 2009.

O'Neill, Jason. *Bitten by the Business Bug: Common Sense Tips for Business and Life from a Teen Entrepreneur.* Las Vegas, NV: CreateSpace Independent Publishing Platform, 2010.

Peterson's. *Teen's Guide to College & Career Planning.* Paramus, NJ: Peterson's, 2011.

Rankin, Kenrya, and Eriko Takada. *Start It Up: The Complete Teen Business Guide to Turning Your Passions into Pay.* San Francisco, CA: Zest Books, 2011.

Schmidt, Eric. *The New Digital Age: Reshaping the Future of People, Nations, and Business.* New York, NY: Knopf, 2013.

Slomka, Beverly. *Teens and the Job Game: Prepare Today—Win It Tomorrow.* Bloomington, IN: iUniverse Star, 2011.

Sommer, Carl. *Teen Success in Career & Life Skills.* Houston, TX: Advance Publishing, 2009.

Thelen, Tom. *Teen Leadership Revolution: How Ordinary Teens Become Extraordinary Leaders.* Las Vegas, NV: CreateSpace Independent Publishing Platform, 2012.

Topp, Carol. *Starting a Micro Business.* Greenville, SC: Ambassador Publishing, 2010.

Vallée, Danielle. *Whiz Teens in Business.* Seattle, WA: Amazon Digital Services, 2008.

Withers, Jennie. *Hey, Get a Job! A Teen Guide for Getting and Keeping a Job.* London, England: Caxton, 2009.

Bibliography

ACTE.com. "What Is CTE?" Retrieved August 18, 2013 (https://www.acteonline.org/general.aspx?id=120#.Uh6j2GRARy-).

The Best Schools. "The 25 Best Entry-Level Jobs." Retrieved August 14, 2013 (http://www.thebestschools.org/blog/2012/01/26/25-entry-level-jobs).

Bureau of Labor Statistics. "Desktop Publishers." Retrieved August 21, 2013 (http://www.bls.gov/ooh/office-and-administrative-support/desktop-publishers.htm).

Bureau of Labor Statistics. "Exploring Career Information from the Bureau of Labor Statistics: 2012-2013 Edition." Retrieved August 14, 2013 (http://stats.bls.gov/k12/index.htm).

Bureau of Labor Statistics. *Occupational Outlook Handbook.* Retrieved August 8, 2013 (http://www.bls.gov/ooh/business-and-financial/home.htm).

Career and Technology Education. "CTE: Learning That Works for America." Retrieved August 4, 2013 (http://www.careertech.org).

Careertech.org. "CTE Vision: Reflect, Transform, Lead—A New Vision for Career Technical Education." Retrieved August 21, 2013 (http://www.careertech.org/career-technical-education/cte-vision.html).

College Startup. "15 Successful Entrepreneurs Who Didn't Need College." Retrieved August 15, 2013 (http://www.college-startup.com/college/15-successful-entrepreneurs-who-didnt-need-college).

Diploma Guide. "eBusiness Associate's and Bachelor's: Degrees at a Glance." Retrieved August 15, 2013 (http://diplomaguide.com/articles/Study_eBusiness_Bachelors_Associate_Online_Degrees_Info.html).

eHow.com. "E-Commerce Manager Job Description." Retrieved August 17, 2013 (http://www.ehow.com/about_6111545_e_commerce-manager-job-description.html).

How Stuff Works. "Business Communications." Retrieved August 21, 2013 (http://money.howstuffworks.com/business-communications).

National Research Center for Career and Technical Education. "Programs of Study." Retrieved August 15, 2013 (http://www.nrccte.org/core-issues/programs-study).

New Castle County Vocational Technical School District. "About Vo-Tech." Retrieved August 18, 2013 (http://www.nccvotech.com/parents-prospective-students).

Niederberger, Mary. "Once Called Vo-tech Schools, Today's Tech Centers Stress That They're Not for Underachievers." August 26, 2010. Retrieved August 17, 2013 (http://www.post-gazette.com/stories/local/neighborhoods-south/once-called-vo-tech-schools-todays-tech-centers-stress-that-theyre-not-for-underachievers-261150).

Rochelle, Christine. "Five Career Prospects for People with a Business Associate's Degree." June 30, 2012. Aol Jobs. Retrieved August 8, 2013 (http://jobs.aol.com/articles/2010/06/30/business-associates-career-prospects).

Sentz, Rob. "2012's Best-Performing Jobs for Associates Degrees." Emsi.com, May 7, 2012. Retrieved August 9, 2013 (http://www.economicmodeling.com/2012/05/07/2012s-best-performing-jobs-for-associate-degrees).

Stover, Del. "The New Vo-Tech." American School. Retrieved August 24, 2013 (http://www.asbj.com/MainMenuCategory/Archive/2013/August/The-New-Vo-Tech.html).

Tooft Design. "10 Richest People Who Didn't Finish College." Retrieved August 18, 2013 (http://www.tooft.com/10-richest-people-who-didnt-finish-college).

Top Ten Reviews. "Computer Programmers." Retrieved August 18, 2013 (http://vocational-careers.toptenreviews.com/computer-programmers-review.html).

U.S. News and World Report. "Paying for College." Retrieved August 8, 2013 (http://www.usnews.com/education/best-colleges/paying-for-college).

Utah State Office of Education. "Preparing Students for the World of Business." Retrieved August 7, 2013 (http://www.schools.utah.gov/cte/business.html).

Virginia's CTE Resource Center. "Career Development." Retrieved August 8, 2013 (http://www.cteresource.org/featured/career_development.html).

Votech Direct Hands-on Programs for Rewarding Careers. "Business." Retrieved August 4, 2013 (http://votechdirect.com).

Wake County Public School System. "Career and Technical Education." Retrieved August 19, 2013 (http://www.wcpss.net/what-we-teach/programs/cte.html).

Index

About the Author

Adam Furgang is a writer who specializes in the middle school and high school educational market. His books include topics such as nutrition, the environment, health and disease, and science. He attended the High School of Art and Design, a vocational high school in Manhattan. He lives in upstate New York with his wife and two sons.

Photo Credits

Cover (figure) Bevan Goldswain/Shutterstock.com; cover (background), pp. 1, 3 Photographee.eu/Shutterstock.com; cover (tablet), interior pages (graph and data sheet) Jirsak/Shutterstock.com; p. 5 Imaginechina/AP Images; p. 8 Monkey Business Images/Shutterstock.com; p. 10 © iStockphoto.com/desperado; p. 13 allesalltag/Alamy; p. 16 Dean Drobot/Shutterstock.com; p. 18 Dragon Images/Shutterstock.com; pp. 21, 36, 63 Goodluz/Shutterstock.com; p. 25 Richard G. Bingham II/Alamy; pp. 28–28, 39 bikeriderlondon/Shutterstock.com; p. 30 Kenishirotie/Shutterstock.com; pp. 32–33 © iStockphoto.com/Bill Oxford; p. 43 JMiks/Shutterstock.com; p. 44 © iStockphoto.com/actual size; p. 46 Bloomberg/Getty Images; p. 50 © iStockphoto.com/GlobalStock; p. 52 © David Grossman/Alamy; p. 55 auremar/Shutterstock.com; pp. 56–57 Michal Kowalski/Shutterstock.com; p. 60 Lisa F. Young/Shutterstock.com; p. 65 Hill Street Studios/Blend Images/Getty Images; cover and interior design elements schab/Shutterstock.com (text highlighting), nikifiva/Shutterstock.com (stripe textures), Zfoto/Shutterstock.com (abstract curves); back cover graphics ramcreations/Shutterstock.com, vectorlib.com/Shutterstock.com.

Designer: Michael Moy; Editor: Shalini Saxena;
Photo Researcher: Cindy Reiman